HOW TO OPERATE A COMPENSATION COMMITTEE

MARC ROSENBERG, CPA

MONOGRAPHS BY MARC ROSENBERG

CPA Firm Management & Governance

CPA Firm Succession Planning: A Perfect Storm

Strategic Planning and Goal Setting For Results

How to Negotiate a CPA Firm Merger

How to Bring in New Partners

What Really *Makes CPA Firms Profitable?*

Guide to Planning the Firm Retreat

Effective Partner Relations and Communications

For more information or to purchase additional titles visit:
www.rosenbergassoc.com + click on
"Monographs by Marc Rosenberg

Connect with Marc:
marc@rosenbergassoc.com
blog.rosenbergassoc.com

HOW TO OPERATE A COMPENSATION COMMITTEE

MARC ROSENBERG, CPA

Copyright ©2013
The Rosenberg Associates Ltd.
1000 Skokie Boulevard, Suite 555
Wilmette, IL 60091

TABLE OF CONTENTS

TABLE OF CONTENTS

1

Introduction

The allocation of partner income is much more an art than a science. Anyone who thinks otherwise is either naïve or has never been a partner whose income is subjected to an allocation process.

Partners are highly skilled professionals who work very hard at what they do. The compensation that a partner earns is essentially a "grade" for performance and overall contribution to the firm.   One's compensation puts a value on each partner's worth to the firm. So it should come as no surprise that of all the CPA firm management practices , there is nothing more sensitive than the allocation of income among the partners.

It's understandable that there is a fair amount of unhappiness, frustration and yes, conflict among partners over their compensation. The sensitivity lies not in the selection of a <u>system</u> used by a firm to allocate income. Instead, the sensitivity arises because of the <u>competitiveness</u> between the partners over their respective compensation levels.   Andrew Grove, the former chairman of Intel, said it best:

> "If people are concerned about their absolute level of compensation, then they <u>can</u> be satisfied. However, if their focus is on relative standing, then they can <u>never</u> be satisfied."

This quote is particularly applicable to partners in accounting firms. Many partners I've encountered came from relatively humble backgrounds and socio-economic status. They earn many times what their parents earned. When they look at their W-2's each year, a smile comes across their faces because they never dreamed their income would reach this level. (In 2012, the average partner of a local, multi-partner firm earned $350,000 to $450,000).

But that proud smile can quickly turn to a frown. All it takes is finding out that another partner – believed to be far less valuable to the firm than oneself – has received a higher income allocation. It's no wonder that partner compensation is such a sensitive topic.

Why is a firm's income allocation system an _art_ rather than a _science_?

1. There has never been a system invented that can be considered 100% fair and just to all the partners. Some firms sarcastically state that the acid test of a good system is one in with which all the partners are a little unhappy.

2. There are three main factors to consider in designing a firm's partner compensation system:

    a. _Objective_ factors which are easy to measure. Most are production oriented and include business origination, book of business, billable hours, realization and age of WIP and A/R.

    b. _Subjective_ factors, which consists of intangible aspects of performance such as firm management, teamwork, loyalty, leadership, work ethic, etc.

c. <u>Partners' capital investment in the firm</u> is the final major category that influences many firm's income allocations, though its impact is usually much lower than the previous two items.

Balancing the allocation of income between these three factors is not easy and fraught with complexity. That's why the delicate handling of partner compensation is considered an art rather than a science.

<u>The evolution of partner compensation</u>

The art of partner compensation has evolved significantly over time. Many years ago, the vast majority of firms tried to keep the system a science by devising a seemingly infinite number of algebraic formulas to allocate income. Virtually all of the factors used in the formula were production metrics. Very few if any intangible factors were included in the system. A crucial element of these systems was the manner in which each factor in the equation was weighted against each other.

But over time, the philosophy of managing CPA firms changed. Firms discovered that formula systems were inadequate because they largely ignored intangible performance factors. Measuring these intangibles defied incorporation into nice, neat formulas. More diverse and sophisticated systems were needed.

As a result, systems were developed that are effective at addressing <u>both</u> production as well as intangible and interpersonal factors. The two most common systems for this are the Compensation Committee and the Managing Partner Decides systems.

The 7 most common CPA partner compensation systems

System	Pros	Cons
Compensation committee - a small number of partners collaborate to allocate income based on their judgment.	Balances production with intangibles. Easier to link pay with goals.	Lack of partner trust. Failure by CC to communicate with the partners could doom the system.
Formula-an algebraic formula that computes each partner's income. Main parts to the formula are Finding, Minding and Grinding.	CPAs like numbers and formulas. It's objective. Avoids quarrels.	Can cause hording. Bad for teamwork. No credit for intangibles. "I" vs. "We" thinking.
Paper & Pencil – each partner votes to allocate income to all partners, including him/herself. The "ballots" are averaged to arrive at an income allocation.	What could be fairer than a system that collectively assesses the value and contributions of every partner? Avoids arguments.	Hard to know how your partners really perform. Partners may not vote properly. Cliques. Narrows gap from high to low.
Ownership pct – income allocated by ownership percentage.	Common way to pay shareholders of other businesses.	Only through a quirk of fate does owner % match performance.
MP decides- the MP allocates income using his best judgment.	Balances production with intangibles. Easier to link pay with goals.	Partners won't give this power to one person. MP often reduces his own pay.
All paid equally.	Easy. No arguments. Teamwork.	Unfair. Demotivating. Encourages coasting.
All partners decide.	Same as Paperslip.	Chaos!!

Partner compensation systems: Usage by size of firm*

	2 Ptrs	3-4 Ptrs	5-7 Ptrs	8-12 Ptrs	13+ Ptrs	All Firms
Comp Comm	0%	19%	23%	54%	70%	32%
Formula	23%	36%	36%	29%	11%	30%
Paper & Pencil	3%	4%	5%	2%	2%	3%
Owner Percent	10%	4%	6%	2%	8%	5%
MP Decides	12%	11%	12%	6%	9%	10%
Pay Equal	32%	6%	4%	4%	0%	7%
All Decide	20%	20%	14%	3%	0%	13%
Open	98%	82%	81%	65%	49%	77%
Closed	2%	18%	19%	35%	51%	23%

Here is a summary of the movement by firms over the past 6 years, TO the compensation committee and AWAY from formulas*:

	5-7 Partners		8-12 Partners		13+ Partners	
	2011	2005	2011	2005	2011	2005
Comp Comm	23%	19%	54%	39%	70%	58%
Formula	36%	47%	29%	39%	11%	38%
All Other	41%	34%	17%	22%	19%	4%

* From a very recent Rosenberg MAP Survey.

As partner compensation systems grew in complexity over time, three subjective systems for allocating income become more common:

1. The <u>managing partner</u> allocates the income based on his/her judgment of what is fair.

2. <u>All the partners decide together</u> how to allocate income. One system devised to do this is the "Paper and Pencil" system. This is a system in which each partner votes to allocate income to all partners, including him/herself, and the "ballots" are averaged to arrive at an income allocation. The thinking is: what could be fairer than a system that collectively assesses the value and contributions of every partner?

3. A <u>compensation committee</u> consists of a small number of partners that allocate the income based on their collective judgment. They function as judges, impaneled for the sole purpose of allocating income.

Today, far and away, the compensation committee has emerged as the system of choice among multi-partner firms, especially those with 8 or more partners.

This monograph focuses on the compensation committee system to allocate partner income.

The dreaded "smoke-filled back room"

To some partners, the term "compensation committee" (CC) conjures up all sorts of negative images, fueling a fair amount of anxiety over adoption of this system, despite partners' acknowledgement of the system's merits on an intellectual level.

The term "smoke-filled back room" has long been used as a term to describe a cabal of powerful, well-connected, cigar-smoking men who meet privately, and usually secretly, to nominate a political candidate without regard for the will of the public. As a life-long Chicagoan, this author has certainly observed this term's usage in the way political decisions are made in the Windy City. New York, Boston and other cities have equal reputations for smoke-filled back rooms.

There is a natural tendency for CCs to be seen by the partners as "smoke-filled back rooms." Part of the problem is perception but unfortunately, part is due to the reality that many CCs fail to communicate to their partners how they work. And as we will see throughout this monograph, communication between the CC and the individual partners is critical to the success of the CC and its acceptance by the partners.

A related fear of a CC is the dreaded word "subjective." The overarching definition of a CC is that it is a subjective system rather than an objective system. Unfortunately, many partners define "subjective" as biased, unfair, one-sided and self-serving. But in the context of a CC allocating partner income, "subjective" should be considered a strength of the system rather than something "bad." If a CC functions correctly, "subjective" means that the committee members have given careful, studied, objective and unbiased consideration to all facts and information relevant to assessing each partner's performance.

2

Basics of
Partner Compensation

The first question a firm must address when selecting a partner compensation system is: Will the system be performance-based or <u>non</u>-performance-based?

<u>What is "performance-based?"</u>

A performance-based partner compensation system is one in which partner income is allocated primarily on how well each partner performs. "Performance" includes many criteria, primarily bringing in business, client billing responsibility, billable hours, firm management, leadership, helping staff grow and advance and numerous intangibles such as teamwork and loyalty.

The central philosophies of a performance-based system are:

- "As the partners go, so goes the firm." Firms' success and profitability is heavily dependent on the partners' performance. Staff performance is important, but it's dwarfed by the partners who bring in 99% of the clients, manage the bulk of client relationships, manage the firm and manage the staff. When the partners do these things well, the firm performs at a high level.

- The best performers thrive on success. Achieving high levels of performance acts like an elixir to these partners, but it must be accompanied by a high level of compensation for it to have full effect. They crave the satisfaction that comes from great accomplishments and hard work.

- Performance-based systems encourage each partner to perform well *every year*. Few firms can afford to have their partners coast on past accomplishments.

- Firms need their partners to come to work *every day* with the mentality that if they don't do something to make money for the firm, nobody else will. Performance-based compensation rewards this attitude.

- If the better performers are paid the same as the weaker performers, there is little incentive for the better performers to excel and a great deal of incentive for the weaker performers to slack off.

A system needn't be 100% performance-based to be considered as such, but the vast majority of the factors used to allocate income should depend on partners' performance. For example, if 80-90% of the factors used to allocate income *are* performance-based and 10-20% is allocated on ownership percentage (a non-performance-based factor), this system would still be considered performance-based.

According to the latest Rosenberg survey, 90% of all systems at firms with three or more partners are *performance-based*; 10% are *non performance-based.*

Three types of **non**-performance-based systems used by CPA firms

1. **All partners paid equally**. This is the Three Musketeers approach –"one for all; all for one." The justification for paying everyone equally is this:

   "We are all good CPAs that work hard and contribute to the success of the firm. Each of us brings different talents to the firm, all of which are valuable. Each year, some of us have better years than others, but in the long term, it evens out. Splitting income equally builds teamwork because we all focus on doing what's best for the firm and are never competitive with each other. We have no arguments about who should be paid more because we all earn the same."

2. **Pay based on relative ownership percentage**. If Smith is a 70% owner and Jones is a 30% owner, then they split the income 70-30. There is a certain amount of logic in this system because in many businesses, profits are split based on ownership percentage.

   Businesses that split income on ownership percentage are often one or both of the following:

   - They are capital-intensive. Examples are manufacturing and real estate companies. Owners with huge sums of money invested in their company and/or huge amounts of capital at risk are entitled to a return on their investment commensurate with the size of their investment.

- They are passive investments in which the owners do not manage the investment. An example would be a mutual fund.

But CPA firms are different. They are not capital-intensive and the income of the firm arises from the day to day work of the partner-owners. The profit derived by the owners is almost totally unrelated to the size of their investment in the firm.

Another reason why it's unfair to use ownership percentage to allocate income is this: I often ask partners how their ownership percentage got to where it is. Most can't give an explanation. Their ownership percentage is a hodgepodge of a number that has increased and decreased numerous times as partners have come and gone. It never was and never will be a valid, fair measure of the relative performance of the partners. I have developed this quote a number of years ago that says it all:

> It's only through a quirk of fate that a partner's ownership percentage is in line with how he/she performs compared to other partners.

There is very little justification for using ownership percentage to allocate income.

There are two important exceptions to this:

- Some firms change each partner's ownership percentage each year to align this number with relative partner performance. These firms occasionally describe their system in practice management surveys as "ownership percentage" but they really practice the compensation committee approach.

- To the extent that ownership percentage is an indicator of the amount of capital each partner has invested in the firm, it's fair that partners should receive a return on their investment. That's why firms carve out a tier of income known as "interest on capital." For 99% of all firms, this interest tier is a very small – usually under 10% - percentage of total partner income.

3. **Partners paid based on seniority.** An antiquated system that has not been a major factor in CPA firm partner compensation for many decades. Justifications for a seniority-based system include:

   - It fosters loyalty, retention, and stability.
   - No arguments about compensation; partners don't get competitive with each other their compensation.
   - For many partners, the more experience they amass the more knowledgeable and proficient they become. This justifies paying someone more the longer they serve as a partner.

The few times I have encountered this system, the tier of income based on seniority usually limits the number of years that one is credited for years as a partner. Example: Each partner earns 5% for each year as a partner, up to a maximum of 20 years.

Virtually all CPA firms totally reject seniority as a valid criterion for allocating partner income. The partners see this as a system similar to the tenure system used in academia, which they despise. Partners have long recognized that the number of years someone is a partner has no bearing on the value of their contributions to the firm.

I have heard a small number of firms admit that, in situations where it is unclear how to differentiate between the performances of two or more partners, *some* consideration of seniority may creep into the decision-making process. But the impact of this is always relatively minor.

Why partner compensation systems should be performance-based

1. To motivate the partners to produce and perform well because they know that they will be fairly and handsomely rewarded for their contributions to the firm's success. If a partner works hard to achieve his/her goals and get paid the same amount as a partner who is a low achiever, it's only natural for the achiever to ask "why bother?"

2. To enable firms to communicate their value system to the partners.

3. To discourage complacency. If a firm achieves success and then, the partners sit back and coast, stagnation inevitably sets in, accompanied by process inefficiencies, which leads to the exodus of clients and staff and ultimately, lower profitability. Firms need every one of their partners to be striving for more every year.

4. Non-performance-based systems are not fair to the partners and do not foster the firm's goals of growth, success and profitability. They rarely match compensation with contributions to success. Whenever anything in life is unfair, people get discouraged and depressed. Partners in a CPA firm are no exception.

5. It's one of several ways, and a powerful way indeed, of achieving a very important but elusive quality of a successful CPA firm – partner accountability.

Best Practices for ALL partner compensation systems

1. The system should be <u>performance-based</u>; there should be a link between pay and performance.

2. <u>Practice development</u> must play a meaningful role. Bringing in business wins everyone's award for the most important aspect of partner performance that partners dislike and would prefer to avoid. So, firms need to provide incentives for partners to go outside their comfort zones to perform this critically important duty.

3. The system should <u>integrate strategic planning</u> with partner compensation; firms need to <u>motivate partners</u> to do what the firm <u>needs</u> them to do.

4. <u>Teamwork rules</u>. Partners do what's best for the firm and never "game" the system. Partners work together to satisfy clients first before figuring out how to get paid for it.

5. <u>Multi-tier</u> systems make sense because they compensate partners for three different roles they play: shareholder (via interest on capital), street value (via base or draw) and performance in the current year (via bonus or final distribution).

6. The variable portion of the system should be significant enough to <u>change behavior</u>. The bonus needs to meaningful to get the partners attention. A bonus that is at least 10% of total partner compensation is considered significant by many firms; anything smaller will not incentivize most partners.

7. The system must be perceived as <u>fair</u> by most partners, over time.

> Note: I have heard many firms say that the acid-test of a fair system is one with which all or most partners are unhappy. <u>I reject this.</u> Based on my personal experience in working with hundreds of firms on partner compensation, I feel it is quite feasible and realistic goal for most of the partners to feel the system is fair.

8. The system should <u>not</u> produce results that <u>vary wildly from year to year</u>; partner contributions should be viewed over a 2-3 year period.

9. The <u>managing partner</u> should have <u>more impact</u> in the partner compensation system than the other partners because he/she needs this leverage to hold partners accountable.

10. <u>Reward intangibles</u>. Examples: mentoring and development of staff, firm management, leadership, teamwork, loyalty, developing new markets, living & breathing the firm's core values.

11. <u>Differentiate between leadership, management and administration</u>.

One of the most powerful speeches I have ever heard was by Bob Bunting, long-time MP of west coast powerhouse Moss Adams. He said this:

- Leadership is worth <u>more</u> than your billing rate.
- Management is worth your billing rate.
- Administration is worth <u>less</u> than your billing rate. Administration, though important, can be done by a person who earns far less than a partner.

Don't pay partners a partner's compensation level (say $350,000 to $450,000) for doing the job of a firm administrator, who typically earns $75,000 to $150,000.

12. Be flexible; change with the times and the firm's needs.

13. For firms of 5-6 partners or more, the compensation committee system is the best way to practice all of the above.

14. Communication of how the system works is critical. Partners should know what's expected of them, how they can make more money and how their allocated income number was determined.

15. Closed vs. open system. Partners at most local firms stubbornly cling to their "inalienable right" to know what their other partners earn, but it makes the job of the compensation committee more difficult when the system is open. More on this in a later chapter.

The most common allocation factors used in partner compensation systems

1. Interest on capital.

2. Production metrics:
   a. Finding- bringing in business.

   b. Minding- size of a partner's billing responsibility, regardless if self-originated. Many firms refer to minding as "book of business." To "qualify" for minding credit, a partner must manage the client relationship as well as the client engagement.

    c.   Grinding- billable hours worked on clients, regardless if the time is on the partner's own or others' clients.

    d.   Age of receivables and WIP, realization and bad debts.

3. Management stipend. At many firms, certain partners spend more time than others on firm management and admin. This reduces the time they can spend on building their production metrics, which could decrease their income allocation.   To keep them "whole," many firms pay a stipend to these partners for their admin time. Stipends are most common when formulas are used.

4. Intangibles such as teamwork, loyalty, mentoring staff, leadership, management, people skills, etc.

5. Achievement of goals.

6. Fulfilling a role in the firm such as department head, chair of the marketing or personnel committee, office PIC, etc.

7. Home runs- spectacularly successful achievements by a partner that clearly warrant special compensation. Examples include bringing in a huge client and identifying a great merger candidate.

Three tiers of income allocation common to most firms

Instead of allocating all income to the partners as one number for each, many firms break down the income paid to each partner into three tiers:

Tier	Common % of Total Partner Income
I. <u>Return on capital</u>. Compensates partners for being a shareholder. Each partner receives a return on his/her accrual basis capital account. The return should be higher than the prime interest rate, perhaps 3-5% higher.	5-10%
II. <u>Base salary</u>. This represents what each partner brings to the table, each and every day. It is impacted by: • Bringing in business • Managing a client base • Performing billable hours • Ability to command a high billing rate • Ability to motivate and develop staff • Leadership and management role Base salaries are usually set prospectively – at the beginning of the year.	65-85%
III. <u>Incentive Bonus</u>. Rewards unusual accomplishments, performance to goals, hitting home runs, intangibles, etc.	10-30%

3

Why Firms Use Compensation Committees

1. It's the best of several common partner compensation systems for achieving a balance between recognizing traditional production accomplishments and rewarding intangibles.

2. The compensation committee approach aligns the firm's strategic plan and vision with how partners are evaluated and how they are compensated. It motivates partners to produce what the firm *needs* them to produce. At most firms, there is a disconnect between these three functions. But at the better managed firms, they are integrated.

3. People understand that formulas have lots of flaws, rendering them unusable.

4. At larger firms (say, firms with 10 or more partners), there may be too many partners for each of them to know what all the others contribute, so the Paper and Pencil system may not work well.

5. The partners won't trust one person (i.e., the MP) with the responsibility (some would say "power") to allocate income.

6. The MP doesn't want the sole responsibility.

7. It places the decision making process in the hands of credible "judges," which gives a certain amount of comfort to the partners. Partners may not always be 100% in agreement with their income allocation, but at least they know that the judges did their best to determine the allocations fairly.

8. There isn't anything better.

Characteristics of a good compensation committee system

1. The crux of the compensation committee (CC) system for allocating partner income is to place the responsibility for making fair and equitable income allocations with a group of people who are <u>trusted to use their best judgment</u> in making their decisions. No rules. No boundaries. No formulas. Just good, honest, unbiased judgment.

   > "If the people being judged don't trust the judges, the system won't work. Period. " (David Maister)

2. If judgment is the #1 characteristic, #2 must be <u>communication</u>. The rules governing the decisions must be consistent and well understood.

   a. At the beginning of each year, the CC must be crystal clear in communicating how they will evaluate each partner at the end of the year. The partners must understand the rules of the game before they start playing. The partners must understand what behaviors and results will translate to higher income levels and conversely, what will hold them back.

   b. As David Maister has also pointed out, "judgments that are explained are more readily accepted than those that are not."

   After the allocations have been decided, the CC must clarify which aspects of performance caused them to award a higher amount of income to each partner and which aspects of performance held back each partner's income.

c.   "A sincere effort must be made by the judges to collect all pertinent information." (David Maister) In other words, the CC shouldn't meet for an hour or so and wing it. They should study the data very carefully before allocating the income.

2.   A good partner compensation system starts with <u>strategic planning</u>. The best systems are designed to motivate and reward partners for producing what the firm *needs* them to produce. How can you craft a partner compensation system without first deciding what the firm wants to be in 5 years? What the firm *needs* from its partners?

Ideally, the firm should go through the proper process for preparing a strategic plan, complete with a vision statement and statement of core values. This process begins with a rigorous session of brainstorming, continues with the identification of goals needed to achieve the vision, and ends with deciding how the plan will be implemented, including the types of partner accountability that are needed.

Not all firms have the desire or the time to prepare a proper strategic plan. However, ALL firms can and should spend some time together putting together a short list of high impact goals that it requires its partners to accomplish.

4

Comp Committee Decisions To Be Made

<u>The very first decision: What does the firm want the compensation committee to be?</u>

The first thing that needs to be decided by the firm is how the CC will operate: What will be the scope of their authority and responsibility? What is their mandate? Firms have two primary choices:

1. The first type of CC is one that actually makes income allocation decisions. **This is the <u>most</u> common way that CCs operate and will, for the most part, is the subject of this monograph**. There are two main sub-types:

    *   The partner group decides to have a CC make income allocation decisions, but within a framework decided by the partner group as a whole. Examples of "framework" are:

        i.   <u>The firm decides</u> if it wants a formula, but the CC is responsible for *devising* the formula, tweaking the formula and making the computations.

        ii. <u>The firm decides</u> the <u>size</u> of each tier of income such as interest, base and bonus.

  iii. <u>The firm decides</u> to allocate the base using a formula and let the CC's judgment determine how the bonus is allocated. The CC's role with the base is limited to simply "running the numbers" and completing a spreadsheet.

- The partner group gives the CC <u>complete authority</u> to make all compensation decisions, with no limitations. So, examples of what the CC might decide are:

  i. What the income tiers will be.
  ii. The size of each income tier.
  iii. The system used to allocate income such as a formula, paper and pencil or subjective collaboration, or some combination.
  iv. Whether or not partners will have goals.
  v. Whether or not there will be performance evaluations of the partners.
  vi. The actual income allocation decisions for each partner.

2. A second type of CC is one in which the firm knows it wants to change its present compensation system and creates an ad-hoc committee to research alternatives and make recommendations to the full partner group. At least initially, the firm has no intention of having the CC actually make income allocation decisions. The CC may have a continuing role in future years to carry out research directed by the partners and make recommendations.

This is the <u>least</u> common scenario used by firms, but a fair number of firms elect to use their CC in this manner.

Compensation committee decisions

Once the firm has decided the scope of authority, power and expectations of the CC, per the previous pages, the following decisions need to be made, either by the partner group as a whole, or by the CC:

1. If the committee is to be appointed, decide when this will be done. If the committee will be elected, decide when elections will be held and set dates for the election.

2. Decide how many members will be on the CC, including the MP.

3. Decide the term of office of CC members. Terms should be staggered so that a minimum number of members leave the committee each year.

4. Should the CC and the executive committee be the same or separate?

5. What performance criteria will the CC use to evaluate the partners?

6. Decide whether the CC will function as management or if it will be strictly limited to allocating the income. If the former, the main "management" part of their job could include some or all of the following:
    - Decide on the performance criteria for partners in the firm.
    - Coordinate the goal setting process, meeting with the partners, and approving their goals.

7. Decide what the structure of partner compensation should be. Should it include some or all of the following tiers, and, what percentage of total partner income should go into each tier?

- Interest on capital. What rate? Should the interest be on accrual or cash basis capital?
- Base salary and/or draw?
- Bonus and/or final distribution?
- Other?

8. If both a base and a bonus:

- Will the base be determined separately from the bonus such that the bonus will be a true <u>incentive</u> bonus?
- Will the base really be a draw on one final number such that the bonus is really a final distribution that trues up each partner's total income for the year?

9. If the base is independent of the bonus, to what extent will some or all of the following impact the base?
- Origination
- Client base managed
- Billable hours and dollars
- Realization
- Management of A/R and WIP
- Official internal duties (MP, EC member, CC member, department head, PIC, etc.)
- Ownership percentage
- Intangibles (teamwork, mentoring of staff, following firm policies, etc.)
- Other

10. If the bonus is independent of the base, to what extent will some or all of the following impact the bonus?
- Achieving or exceeding goals.
- What each partner did to enable the firm to have a good year (bad year).
- Intangibles.
- No guidelines; solely at the discretion of the CC.

11. Decide how each partner's progress on goals will be <u>monitored</u> throughout the year and who will do it.

12. Will the firm use the paper and pencil method as a non-binding source of information for the CC? Will this be done for both the base and bonus? Who will tabulate it?

13. What information will the CC review to form its evaluation of each partner?   Possible examples include:

  - Production statistics such as Finding, Minding, Grinding, realization, WIP and A/R management.
  - Evaluations of the partners:
      i.   Self-evaluation
      ii.   Peer evaluation
      iii. Upward evaluation by the staff
      iv.   Client satisfaction survey
      v.   Performance appraisal conducted by a partner's supervisor
  - Achievement of formal, written goals.
  - Performing appropriate role in the firm.
  - Input from members of management that are not on the CC such as PICs and department heads.
  - Non-binding paper and pencil exercise.
  - Assessment of the extent that each partner lived and breathed the firm's core values.
  - Anything else the CC considers relevant.

14. What will be the reporting year for the above data?
  - If your firm is a calendar year-end:
      i.   When will the committee deliberate? Data won't be available until the 3rd week or so of January. The CC needs time to study and review the data, so, their first meeting may not be until the end of January or beginning of February. Is this feasible in the busy season?

ii. An alternative is to prepare the data on a basis other than a calendar year-end. An example would be November 1 through October 31 or December 1 through November 30.

- If the firm is NOT a calendar year-end, are you comfortable having goals and compensation being done on a basis other than calendar year-end?

15. How will the CC members actually make their decisions?

- The MP makes an initial recommendation, which is then discussed and finalized as a committee, or,
- The CC has a discussion and reaches a group consensus.
- Other.

16. Determining the compensation of the CC members:
- Will each CC member's compensation be dealt with the same as any other partner?
- Will each CC member leave the room as he/she is discussed?

17. Communication: How will the CC communicate with each partner:

- Will the CC meet with each partner at the beginning of the year to communicate the guidelines that will be used at the end of the year to determine his/her compensation?
- Will the CC meet one or more times during the year to monitor progress on goals?
- After the income allocations are completed at year-end, how will the CC communicate to each partner the factors used to determine his/her income?

18. Will the system be open or closed? In an open system, all partners know all partners' income. In a closed system, only CC members know what each partner earns.

19. Appeal procedures?
    - Appeals allowed with possibility of adjusting the numbers?
    - No appeals; decisions of the CC are final (partners always entitled to a "hearing").

20. Approvals required of CC decisions?
    - Yes, by full partner group.
    - Yes, by management/executive committee.
    - No, CC decisions are final.

5

The Judges

The heart and soul of the Compensation Committee (CC) method for allocating partner income is this:

> "The system can only work if the people being judged are willing to trust the judges. Period. If the partners aren't comfortable with this, then they should not use the CC." (David Maister)

The following is from an article entitled "The Ideal Judge," which featured quotations from a South African Chief Justice, M.M. Corbett. Despite the article's obvious intent to describe the ideal qualities of a courtroom judge, the parallels to a CC member are striking.

Said Corbett: "If I were to attempt to sum up in half-a-dozen words the qualities which ideally a judge should have, I would say *knowledge, experience, judgment, independence, character,* and *industry."*

Knowledge and experience. "He must have the knowledge and experience of the world and its way to make a good assessment of the probabilities and to weigh them correctly; he must be endowed with common sense."

Judgment: "It relates to both the fact-finding and to the application of the law to the facts. A judge must have the skill to arrive at the truth, for many more cases are decided on the facts than on the law."

Independence. "The judge must be not only willing but also unflinching in his resolve to decide cases in whatever way his professional skills and his conscience direct him, whatever the consequences and however unpopular his decision may be. He must be objective, unbiased, unattached to any preconceived notions or philosophy which would tend to make him take sides, to take an unduly severe or an unduly lenient view of certain types of conduct."

Character. "The Judge must have the personality to maintain order and dignity in court proceedings."

Industry. "Judges must be extremely industrious. They have to not only work for long hours, often in the evenings and over weekends, but they have to see to it that they produce with minimum delay what the parties have come for. To these qualities I would add only humility and the ability to express himself with reasonable clarity."

What are the ideal qualities of a CC member? A good list would include the following, all of which relate to at least one of the six qualities above:

1. Be fair and unbiased. Avoid any perception of being self-serving.

2. Recognize both results and efforts.

3. Evaluate how each partner performed vs. what was expected.

4. Look at both traditional production (Finding, Minding and Grinding) and intangibles, making sure that one isn't valued so highly as to render the other inconsequential.

5. Avoid being overly conservative:

a.   Be open to rewarding impressive performances from lower paid partners such that they may leap over higher paid partners.

b.   Be willing to scale back the compensation of higher paid partners whose performance is disappointing and fails to justify their historically high compensation levels.

6.   Some partners have reputations for "going ballistic" when they get upset or things don't go their way. A good CC member is willing to recommend compensation amounts to these volatile personalities fully knowing that they may be publicly and vociferously ridiculed by these partners.

7.   In professional sports, players are frequently voted to all-star teams based on their past performance. Present recognition is based on past accomplishments. Many view this as unfair.

When evaluating each partner's performance, there is a natural tendency to "assume" partners perform well in certain areas based on previous accomplishments. For example, a partner who traditionally has been a rainmaker may continue to enjoy this reputation despite several years of hardly bringing in *any* business. CC members should carefully study all data collected and avoid making quick, impulsive judgments or listening to hearsay.

8.   CC members should be prepared to explain and communicate their judgments and decisions, both to the partner group as a whole as well as one-on-one with partners.

6

Make-up of the Compensation Committee

There are 6 aspects of organizing a compensation committee:

1. The Managing Partner is a permanent CC member.
2. The CC should be small.
3. The firm must decide if the CC is to be the same or separate from the executive committee.
4. Every CC member should be credible to the other partners.
5. No mandatory rotation.
6. Terms of CC members and term limits.

1. Managing partner is a permanent member

If the MP is responsible for the overall management of the firm, this must include basic duties that any President or CEO has, including:

1. The growth and profitability of the firm.
2. The firm's strategic direction.
3. The performance of all personnel, including partners.
4. Holding partners accountable for their performance.

The only possible exception to the MP being a permanent member of the CC is this scenario, which is not uncommon at smaller firms: A partner may have the MP title, but he/she functions more as the admin partner or even the firm administrator. This type of MP usually is not responsible for the four duties above. Instead, the focus is on organizing partner meetings, heading up internal accounting, supervising admin staff, maintaining the firm's systems and procedures, etc.

2. The CC should be small

Firms with 7 or fewer partners find it challenging to have a CC. It's logical to have 3 people be on the committee, but firms ask themselves: Does it make sense to have 3 out of 7 partners on the CC? Each firm is different, with different personalities and they should do what make sense to them. I have seen firms with as few as 5 partners function effectively with a two-person CC.

The vast majority of firms with two-person CCs have the following characteristics: The two are clearly (a) senior to the other three and (b) possess much larger books of business than the other three.

A three person CC can continue to serve a firm very well as the total number of partners rises into the mid-teens, perhaps even a tad higher. When a CC of three feels that they don't have enough members to be familiar enough with all the partners' performance, they usually increase the committee size to five to enable it to add partners with management oversight duties such as department heads.

A final factor that impacts the size of the CC is the presence of other offices that are significant in size. Many firms feel that PICs of significantly sized offices should sit on the CC.

3. Should members of the CC and the EC be the same or different?

Executive committee defined. When the number of partners in a firm gets too large to involve all partners on all issues, firms create an Executive Committee (EC) to work with the managing partner on the firm's strategic and high-level governance issues, functioning as a Board. At some point, as firms continue to grow and make more use of the EC, they often decide to convene fewer general partner meetings.

When references are made to the "management" of the firm, this includes the EC.
Some of the more important duties of an EC are:

1. Provide high-level advice and counsel to the managing partner.
2. Provide assistance to the MP as needed, including managing the performance of other partners.
3. Brainstorm with the MP about various strategic issues and the direction of the firm.
4. Initiate preliminary merger discussions.
5. Address sensitive and confidential personnel problems.

Should the CC = EC? Three schools of thought.

1. Members of the EC and the CC should be the same.

2. The EC and CC members should be separate.

3. Some members should be on both and some should be separate.

In reading the following arguments for each school of thought, it's important to understand that the managing partner should be an automatic member of both committees.

Why the EC and CC should be comprised of the <u>same</u> partners.

If a partner - whether it's the MP, EC member, PIC or department head - has responsibility for managing the performance and behavior of other partners, he/she needs to be able to link the compensation of those individuals with their performance. Firms that adhere to this school of thought endow their EC with the duty to allocate partner income.

1. Most of the world works this way: The boss determines pay of his/her reports. Management is in the trenches working with the partners 365 days a year on their performance, so, they know best.

    Therefore, <u>management</u> should have the ability to link pay with performance and not have it handled by a "jury" that only spends a few days a year allocating income and lacks the intimate familiarity with each partners' performance.

2. If a management partner supervises other partners, and works with a partner on his/her opportunities and shortcomings all year, this partner may <u>not</u> make the necessary commitment to heed the supervising partner's

direction because he/she knows that a separate CC, not the supervising partner, will determine his/her pay.

3. Putting non-management partners on the CC turns the compensation process into a "jury." In a period that lasts just several days, the CC , despite their best efforts, can't possibly become familiar enough with each partners' performance to be effective and fair at allocating income.

Why the EC and CC should be <u>separate</u>.

1. Democracy is often a powerful influence on how firms govern. Having separate committees provides the firm with a system of checks and balances, a fundamental doctrine of democratic governments. Proponents of the separation approach are concerned that making the two committees the same will vest too much power in the EC.

2. It gives more partners an opportunity to be part of management, regardless of which committee they serve on. Cynics would say that these firms feel it's more important to give everyone a chance than for the committee to function effectively.

3. It's important to keep management out of the income allocation process because:

    a. This prevents them from being vindictive.
    b. Non-management partners will be more objective in allocating income.

A compromise approach: Create <u>overlap</u>.

With this approach, some partners are on <u>both</u> committees and some are only on <u>one</u> committee. This satisfies both lines of thinking.
Examples:

- Assume the EC and CC each has 3 members. The MP is on both committees. One other EC member serves on the CC and a non-EC partner serves on the CC.

- All 3 EC members serve on the CC. In addition, one additional non-EC partner serves on the CC.

4. <u>Every member of the CC must be credible in the eyes of the other partners.</u>

CC members can be appointed by the MP or elected by the partners. Regardless of the selection method, all committee members must be seen by the other partners as having the six characteristics of good judges listed in Chapter 4:
- Knowledge.
- Experience.
- Judgment.
- Independence.
- Character.
- Industry.

Put another way, all CC members MUST be credible in the eyes of the other partners. Many firms have a very productive, competent partner that the others are glad to call "partner," yet, because of the nature of this person's personality or perhaps due to some past transgressions, the others don't wish to entrust their compensation with this person.

5. <u>No mandatory rotation</u>.

   As stated earlier, many firms are driven by a commitment to democracy in structuring their governance. This causes some firms to feel that, to be fair, and perhaps to adhere to the "checks and balances" theory, every partner should get a chance to serve on the CC. This can be a mistake because many firms have at least one partner who would not be seen as credible by the other partners. Eventually, this partner would be on the CC and that's when the credibility of the CC itself falls into question.

   If a CC member is doing a good job, why require him/her to drop off the committee?

6. <u>Term limits of CC members.</u>

   Most firms stipulate a two or three year term for CC members. It's very important to stagger the terms of CC members so that there is continuity from year to year.

   Most firms stop short of requiring that every partner be given a chance to serve on the CC, but some like to limit the number of consecutive terms to two or three. These firms usually allow a partner to come back on the CC after they have been off for a year.

44

7

Assessing Partner Performance

<u>Ways to assess partner performance</u>

To address this issue, a firm has to decide which one of these two models it will follow:

1. The firm is driven first, by its strategic plan and vision. Partner production is important, but it is secondary to strategic planning.

2. The firm will always be driven by partner production because that's how a firm makes money. Strategic planning is important, but it is secondary to partner production.

To be honest, as a veteran consultant to CPA firms for over 20 years, I must tell you that the vast majority of firms under $10-15 million are partner production driven, not strategic planning driven. Some firms may *say* or *think* they are strategic planning driven, but they really only give it lip service.

The extent to which a firm is one or the other of these two alternatives goes a long way to determining how partner performance will be assessed:

- If a firm is <u>strategic planning driven</u>, the assessment process will place a great deal of importance on what each partner did to help the firm achieve its strategic goals and vision. There will be a lot of emphasis on partner goal setting. To these firms, it's very important that the partners do what the firm *needs* them to do.

- If a firm is <u>partner production driven</u>, the assessment process will focus on Finding, Minding and Grinding metrics. These firms are less likely to have a partner goal setting program. Helping the firm achieve its strategic goals will fall into the "nice to have" category, but will play a minor role in assessing a partner's performance.

<u>Management philosophy flowchart: The link between strategic planning and partner compensation</u>

I've been using the flowchart on the next page for 20 years, and it has withstood the test of time. All CPA firms operate at least partially as illustrated by this flowchart. There are five levels, starting at the top:

1. **The bus.** Jim Collins, in his *Good to Great* book, wrote that "before a firm begins strategic planning, it must get the right people ON the bus and the wrong people OFF the bus." Before beginning strategic planning, negative people must leave the firm, or at least, be muted.

2. **The vision**. Everything starts with a vision. What does the firm want to look like in 5 or 10 years?

3. **Firm goals.** The next step is to decide what firm-wide goals are needed to achieve the vision. Example: If the vision is to double in size in 5 years, a firm goal might be to create a marketing plan.

4. **Partner goals.** This is the first stage where a firm breathes life into its strategic plan. The "firm" can't produce any results until specific people or teams are assigned to each of the firmwide goals.

CPA FIRM MANAGEMENT FLOWCHART

Get the <u>right</u> people ON the bus and get the <u>wrong</u> people OFF the bus.

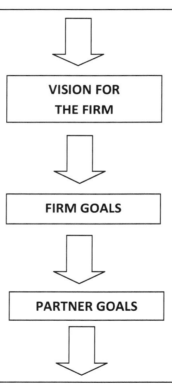

VISION FOR
THE FIRM

FIRM GOALS

PARTNER GOALS

ENGINES (IMPLEMENTATION)

- LEADERSHIP (CHAMPION)
- MANAGEMENT STRUCTURE
- ACCOUNTABILITY
- PARTNER COMPENSATION

5. **The engines.** Prior to the "engines" level of the flowchart, the steps preceding it are like a car whose ignition has yet to be turned on. The four engines turn the car on and keep it going:

    a. Leadership. Every plan needs a champion. Without this champion, a plan is doomed to fail.

    b. Management structure. Line partners are very busy people, taking great care of clients and staff. They need the support of a management structure to help them achieve their strategic goals.

    c. Accountability. Without partner accountability, strategic planning will be a waste of time. There must be accountability for partners achieving their goals.

    d. Partner compensation. Many firms make the mistake of devising a partner compensation system before a vision for the firm is created. How can a firm put together a compensation system if it doesn't know what it needs its partners to achieve?

Partner goal setting

The overarching principle of performance evaluation, for both partners and staff, is establishing expectations up front. It is very difficult if not impossible to properly and fairly evaluate someone's performance if expectations for a person aren't clarified up front.

At the highest level, partners should be evaluated based on the extent to which they achieved their goals and fulfilled their role in the firm. This is a fundamental principle that is elusive to many firms.

As discussed earlier in this chapter, the ideal way to set partner goals is to first create a strategic plan. This way, the firm ensures that the partner goals are in sync with the firm's goals.

The next page shows a template for partner goals. It shows two types of goals: Production and qualitative goals, the latter of which could include strategic planning goals.

INDIVIDUAL PARTNER GOALS FORM

NAME_____

For the Year Ended _____

Production Goals

	Target	Actual
Billing rate		
Business originated		
Client responsibility (also referred to as billing responsibility or book of business)		
Billable hours		
Realization percentage		
Age of WIP		
Age of A/R		

Qualitative goals

Goal	Deadline	Weighting
1.		
2.		
3.		
4.		
Management's discretion		
Total		100%

Six Sources of Partner Goals

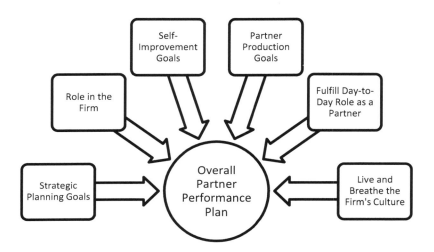

Some firms may not be able to tap into each of the 6 areas.

The Best Goals are SMART Goals

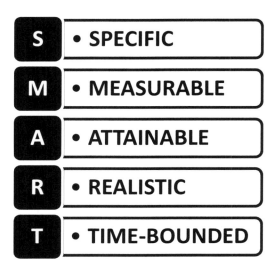

Living and breathing the firm's core values

Certainly, one of the buzz phrases of our time is the importance of partners "living and breathing the firm's core values." That's all well and good, but many firms have not taken the time to formalize exactly what their core values *are*. Here, on one page, is the essence of core values.

Core values defined.

- The attitudes and beliefs that define a firm's culture.
- If our firm were an organized religion, what would our beliefs be and what would constitute a sin?
- Words that influence the way we behave <u>every day.</u>
- The values are used to help people make tough decisions.
- Core values are what we stand for, what we hold dear.
- Violations of core values are never tolerated or ignored.

<u>If the firm's core values are created at a retreat and never seen or talked about thereafter, then their creation was a waste of time.</u>

Good examples of core values.

- Uncompromising commitment to <u>exceed</u> client expectations.
- Clients come first, the firm second and the individual last.
- Everyone required – not just encouraged – to learn new skills.
- Every partner commits to their obligation to mentor staff.
- We accomplish more as a team than any of us could alone.
- Key people find ways to transfer knowledge and expertise to others.
- Partners must set an example for staff to follow.
- Each partner must continually earn the right to remain an owner. Do your share and a little bit more.

52

These "Core Values" are (usually) a waste of time.

Resist the temptation to identify as "core values" those traits that *every* CPA firm would use to describe its values. Examples:

- Ethical
- Responsibility
- Honesty
- Quality
- Integrity
- Excellence
- Diversity
- Professionalism
- Growth

Overall performance criteria for partners

Though more common at firms over $15M, many firms establish a short list of high impact performance criteria against which all partners are evaluated.

- Not all partners will be expected to excel at all criteria.
- Each partner may have a different array of performance criteria.

A good set of performance criteria can be found on the following pages.

Intangible performance attributes for partners

Woven through the partner performance attributes on the next two pages are the following intangible qualities. Firms across the country are paying more and more attention to the importance of these traits because they feel it is more important what partners do with their *non- billable time* than their *billable* time.

1. Mentoring and training of staff.
2. Earning respect and credibility of the partners.
3. Earning respect and credibility of the staff.
4. Delegating work to staff.
5. Gaining the trust of clients.
6. Trustworthy in terms of fiscal matters and making judgments.
7. Acting like an owner, not an employee.
8. Proactive contributor to partner meetings.
9. Technical expertise.
10. Timely adherence to the firm's policies and procedures.
11. Marketing efforts such as speeches, articles and networking.
12. Overall leadership.
13. Teamwork.
14. Management.
15. Loyalty; willingness to incur inconveniences for the firm's benefit.

Partner Performance Criteria

Leadership
- Performance in management positions
- Impacting the behavior & performance of partners & staff
- Having credibility among partners & staff
- Stretching the abilities of others
- Identifying challenges & quickly resolve them
- Getting people to follow

People Skills
- Excellence at managing all relationships
- Mentoring staff and younger partners so they advance
- Inspiring people to achieve

Practice Development
- Emphasis is on how the <u>TEAM</u> performed at bringing in business
- Moving clients upscale in sophistication, profitability and usage of multiple services
- Developing referral sources
- Being active in the community

Client Transition
- Retention
- "If you leave, will clients stay with the firm?"
- Successfully moving clients to other partners
- Transitioning clients in anticipation of retirement
- Transfering expertise

Partner Performance Criteria

Traditional Production Measures
- Traditional production metrics treated the same as other evaluation criteria.
- Examples: business origination, book of business, billable hours and realization

Client Service
- Establishing strong client loyalty
- Attentiveness to the clients' needs
- Strong client retention
- Clients hire the firm for expanded services

Teamwork
- Developing a strong team
- Providing clients with multiple "touch points" within the firm
- Sharing work among business units
- Making inter-unit referrals

Good Citizenship
- Being a good partner
- Treating people respectfully
- Living/breathing firm's core values every day
- Following policies and procedures
- Communicating well with other partners
- Responding timely to emails & voice mails
- Being accountable for performance & behavior

Who should assess the partners' performance?

The answer to this question goes a long way to determining the mandate of the compensation committee. It's quite difficult to separate the income allocation process from performance assessment.

The fundamental question is this: Will the firm's management (the MP and the Executive Committee and to a lesser extent, office PICs and department heads) assess partner performance or will the CC do it?

- If management does the assessment, they give the evaluation results to the CC who allocates the income based on this information. This approach is common at larger firms where management plays a major role in managing partner performance and behavior.

- If management does not do the assessment, then the CC does it first before they allocate income. This approach is common at smaller firms where management does not play a major role in managing other partners. In this scenario, the CC literally becomes part of "management."

8

Partner Base Salary and Bonus

Earlier we described the three tiers of partner income common to most at firms:

1. Interest on capital – provides partners a return on the money they have invested in the firm.

2. Base salary –represents each partner's "street value" to the firm, generally determined by cumulative/historical measures of their performance such as business originated (Finding) and the size of one's client responsibility (Minding).

3. Bonus – a reward for performance in the *current* year; kind of "what have you done for me lately?" This includes achievement of goals.

Two key decisions the firm needs to make

1. Will the base and the bonus be determined *separately* from one another and hence, be mutually exclusive? Or, will the base really be a draw on one final income number, with the bonus serving as a final year-end distribution that trues up the total income number?

2. To what extent will the base be *different* for *each partner* and what methodology will be used to differentiate the base for each partner?

Determining the base for each partner

Larger firms tend to set partner base salaries that are quite different from one another and smaller firms have more of a tendency to have bases that are similar or equal to each other.

Larger CPA firms are generally managed in a more sophisticated manner than smaller firms and as such, emulate corporate world practices, which of course, set bases for their executive officers at levels that vary quite a bit from high to low. Larger CPA firms also follow corporate world methods by embracing the concept of a true incentive bonus where the base and the bonus are mutually exclusive.

Smaller firm practices are much less formal than at larger firms. At smaller firms, it's much more likely for the partners to look at their bases as simply a draw or advance on their final income amounts, determined when the year is completed. As a result, they are comfortable setting the bases/draws at relatively equal amounts because they know that at the end of the year, things will be "trued up."

Evidence of the differences in the compensation of CPA firm partners is found in the annual Rosenberg MAP Survey. Though the following data is from the 2012 survey, the ratios don't change much from year to year. The numbers below are the ratios of the highest paid partner in the firm to the lowest paid partner:

- Firms over $20M: 3.6 to 1
- Firms $10-20M: 2.7 to 1
- Firms $2-10M: 1.9 to 1
- Firms under $2M: 1.4 to 1

Factors that firms consider in setting partner <u>base salaries</u> primarily include:

1. Business originated by each partner during his/her career with the firm that is <u>still with the firm.</u>

2. Client base managed by the partner. Firms should differentiate between two types of partners here:

   a. The partner who originated most or all of his/her client base.

   b. The partner whose client base benefited from transfers to him/her. Transfers include accounts delegated from other partners, clients inherited from retired partners and clients acquired by the firm via merger or purchase.

   It's certainly important for partners to manage their client base effectively, regardless of whether they originated it or not. But few would question the practice of compensating more for originated client base than inherited/transferred client base.

3. Clients transferred by originators to other partners. Firms should avoid blindly looking at a partner's client base managed without checking to see what he/she delegated to other partners. For example, assume a scenario in which a rainmaking partner manages a client base of $1 million, which is higher than 5 of her 8 partners, but lower than two partners with a client base of $1.4M and $1.2M, respectively. Further assume that the partner with the $1M client base *originated* $2.5M, delegating a fair amount of that to the two partners whose client base managed exceeds $1M. Care must be taken to avoid penalizing the rainmaker for having a lower client base managed than the two partners that received her clients.

4. Billable hours that the partner is able to work on a consistent basis, year in and year out.

5. Realization, WIP and A/R management.

6. Leadership and management positions and roles in the firm and the effectiveness of the partners' performance in these roles.

7. Intangibles that each partner brings to the firm year-in and year-out. For examples, if certain partners have a long standing reputation among the other partners for always being willing to assist other partners or being particularly effective at helping staff grow and advance in the firm, this has tremendous value to the firm and must be recognized in setting base compensation.

Determining the bonus for each partner

Firms with bonus tiers that are determined independent of the base often have one or more of the following characteristics:

1. A fairly well developed goal setting program, which plays a big role in the compensation committee's methodology for determining the bonus for each partner.

2. The firm is extremely profitable (say, well in excess of $500,000 per partner). The average *base* salary for their partners may be equal to the *total* compensation for less profitable firms. Therefore, they are able to put more of the total compensation into the bonus pool. We have seen bonus pools for these firms in the range of 25-50% of total compensation.

3. One or more partners slugged a major "home run." Examples: success fee on a client merger, a merger with another CPA firm and bringing in a big client.

Factors that firms consider in setting partner <u>bonuses</u> primarily include:

1. Achievement of formal, written goals.

2. Accomplishments that enabled the firm to have a "good year." For example, if the firm earned partner income of $3M last year and $3.3M this year, the CC needs to study the financial statements and identify what enabled the firm to earn an additional $300,000, and who played big roles in achieving this improvement.

3. Performance in intangibles areas. Readers of this monograph will observe that intangibles are included as criteria for both base and bonus. Intangibles in the base relate more to qualities built up over a lifetime at the firm. Intangibles in the bonus relate more to new things: for example, the firm's star staff person attempts to resign, but is persuaded by one of the partners to withdraw the resignation.

4. Extraordinary performances, including hitting "home runs."

5. Discretionary judgment of the CC.

The CC has two duties at year-end

1. Base salaries and draws are set <u>prospectively</u> for the coming year.
2. Bonuses are set <u>retrospectively</u> for the year just ended.

For a calendar year firm:

*   On January 1, bases are set going forward for the current year:
*   After December 31 of the year, two things are done:
    *   The bonuses for the year just ended are finalized.
    *   The bases for the new year are re-set.

At firms where the base is really a draw on one final number: A common practice for firms in re-setting the base salaries or draws for the <u>upcoming year</u> is to set them in the ratio of total income for each partner in the prior year. See the next two pages for an illustration.

Note: Interest on capital is excluded from this illustration.

<u>Illustration of how base and bonus is actually finalized when</u>
<u>the **base is really a draw** on one final income number</u>

Step 1: Here are the draws that were set <u>prospectively</u> at the beginning of the year:

Jones	450,000	30.0%
Smith	350,000	23.3%
Johnson	300,000	20.0%
Ames	225,000	15.0%
Roberts	175,000	11.7%
Total	**1,500,000**	**100.0%**

Step 2: Finalizing the income allocation for the year just ended, by determining the final distribution:

	Draw	Bonus/ Final Distribution	Total For The Year		Beg. of Year	Change
			Amount	Pct		
Jones	450,000	120,000	570,000	30.0%	30.0%	0.0%
Smith	350,000	68,000	418,000	22.0%	23.3%	-1.3%
Johnson	300,000	99,000	399,000	21.0%	20.0%	1.0%
Ames	225,000	41,000	266,000	14.0%	15.0%	-1.0%
Roberts	175,000	72,000	247,000	13.0%	11.7%	1.3%
Total	**1,500,000**	**400,000**	**1,900,000**	**100.0%**	**100.0%**	**0.0%**

The following can be observed:

- Johnson and Roberts finished the year with a higher income- sharing percentage than they started the year with because their performance for the year merited this increase.
- Smith and Ames finished with a lower income percentage.
- Jones' income percentage did not change.

65

Step 3: Re-set the draws for next year:

The firm decided to increase total draws from $1.5M last year to $1.6M in the current year.

The draws are re-set for each partner based on their final income-sharing percentages for the previous year (see step #2). This results in increases for Jones, Johnson and Roberts while the draws for Smith and Ames remained the same.

	New Draw		Last Year's	Increase
	Amount	Pct.	Draw	(Decrease)
Jones	480,000	30.0%	450,000	30,000
Smith	350,000	22.0%	350,000	-
Johnson	336,000	21.0%	300,000	36,000
Ames	225,000	14.0%	225,000	-
Roberts	209,000	13.0%	175,000	34,000
Total	**1,600,000**	**100%**	**1,500,000**	**100,000**

At firms where the base is <u>independent</u> of the bonus: The most common practice is for the CC to re-set the bases using their best judgment, just as they determined how to allocate the bonus. Some firms re-set the bases in the same manner described in the previous paragraph. See the next two pages for an illustration.

Illustration of how base and bonus is actually finalized when the **base and bonus are independent**

The process is identical to the case illustrated above, except that the CC has the flexibility of re-setting the bases for next year in whatever manner they deem appropriate.

Note: Interest on capital is excluded from this illustration.

Step 1 – Total income last year was $1,700,000.

Step 2 - Bases for this year are:

Cobb	450,000	27.8%
Banks	380,000	23.5%
Musial	340,000	21.0%
Williams	250,000	15.4%
Hornsby	200,000	12.3%
Total	1,620,000	100.0%

Step 3 – The firm finished the year with total profits of $1,920,000, an increase of 12.9% from the prior year. If every partner performed the same in the current year, each would receive an average increase of 12.9%. But Musial & Hornsby had great years, Williams had an average year and Cobb & Banks coasted, so they had so-so years.

	Base	Bonus		Total Income This Year	Total Income Last Year	Pct. Incr.
		Amount	Pct.			
Cobb	450,000	60,000	20.0%	510,000	472,222	8.0%
Banks	380,000	30,000	10.0%	410,000	398,765	2.8%
Musial	340,000	90,000	30.0%	430,000	356,790	20.5%
Williams	250,000	46,200	15.4%	296,200	262,346	12.9%
Hornsby	200,000	73,800	24.6%	273,800	209,877	30.5%
Total	1,620,000	300,000	100.0%	1,920,000	1,700,000	12.9%

Step 4 – Reset bases for next year. Their budget calls for total income of $2,100,000. They decide to set the total bases at $1,700,000, a 4.9% increase over the previous year's base tier. This leaves a target bonus pool of $400,000, $100,000 higher than the previous year's bonus. The CC decided that it wants to build the bonus tier faster than the base tier.

As you review the table below, you will see that Musial and Hornsby received increases to their base considerably higher than the firm's average and higher than the increases of the other partners. This is attributable to their excellent performance in the prior year. Williams received a base increase very close to the overall average because he, in fact, had an average year last year. Finally, Cobb and Banks received a very small increase in their base because they had so-so years.

	Base Last Year	Base This Year		Projected Bonus	Projected Total
		Amount	% Incr.		
Cobb	450,000	455,000	1.1%		
Banks	380,000	385,000	1.3%		
Musial	340,000	370,000	8.8%		
Williams	250,000	260,000	4.0%		
Hornsby	200,000	230,000	15.0%		
Total	1,620,000	1,700,000	4.9%	400,000	2,100,000

9

Collecting Performance Data

As you might suspect, there is no standard list of required data for compensation committees to review. But here is a good, solid list of the basics, which should not only serve as a minimum, but will go a long way towards an optimal collection:

1. Basic production statistics, including Finding, Minding, Grinding, realization and WIP/A/R management data.

2. Input from key members of management who are not compensation committee members. Examples: Office PICs, department heads and administrative professionals such as the COO, marketing director and human resources director.

3. Performance of goals.

4. Partner evaluations performed by management.

5. Self-evaluations by the partners.

6. Upward evaluations of the partners by the staff.

7. Non-binding paper and pencil exercise. This should only be done if the partner group is small enough for each partner to be sufficiently familiar with the performance and behavior of his/her fellow partners. A firm should never use the paper and pencil exercise if the partners are essentially guessing at the performance of other partners.

The reporting year of the data

The key issue here is assessing how the tax season impacts the timing of the compensation committee's work.

Firms with fiscal year-ends won't have any difficulty finding a period of time for the compensation committee (CC) to meet that is free from the burden of the tax season.

Calendar year firms have a natural scheduling conflict with the tax season, which is the most logical time for the compensation committee to meet.

Most firms need the first three weeks in January to finalize the data listed on the previous page. Then, the CC needs a week or so to review and study the data. So, it isn't until the end of January or beginning of February that the CC is ready to deliberate. Unfortunately, this is the time that the tax season heats up in earnest, creating a huge scheduling dilemma for CC members who almost always have substantial client loads.

Firms have three choices for dealing with this conflict:

1. Change the 12 month period of the data reviewed by the CC to a period that ends well in advance of December 31. This could be June 30, September 30 or October 31. This way, the CC process is completed towards the end of the calendar year, thereby freeing the CC members of the conflict with the tax season.

2. Keep the 12 month reporting period on a calendar year-end basis, but the CC doesn't begin its deliberations until after April 15.

3. Keep the 12 month reporting period on a calendar year-end basis, with the CC deliberating during the tax season. Firms that are able to do this either have a relatively light tax season or have partners who don't sleep.

Here is a chart showing the sources of the data used by the CC to evaluate the partners:

Performance measures for the partners	Sources for Evaluating Partner Performance				
	Basic operating stats for the firm	Self Evals*	Partner Evals by mgmt.	MP, PICs, Dept Heads	Upward Evals of partners by staff
Production metrics	X				
Goals achievement	X	X		X	
Fulfilling one's role in the firm		X	X	X	
Satisfaction of core performance criteria for *all* partners		X	X	X	X
Other accomplishments that merit recognition		X		X	X
What each partner did to enable the firm to have a *good* year (or, who held the firm back)	X	X	X	X	
Intangibles		X	X	X	X

* See next page for a sample Self-Evaluation form. Prior to completing a self-evaluation, all partners should receive a summary of key productions statistics such as personal billable hours, client base managed, realization on both, age of WIP, age of A/R, etc.

PARTNER SELF-EVALUATION FORM

Name_____   Date _____

1. Summarize the year you had based on your production statistics. Explain why you think the numbers were good, not good, OK, etc.

   a. Billable hours, including realization

   b. Business brought in, both from new clients and cross-selling to existing clients.

   c. The size of the client base you managed, including retention of clients. Include clients that you transferred to others and therefore, are no longer on your billing run.

2. Looking at the production statistics, do they tell the full story for what you contribute to the firm? If not, give examples of why not. Explain unusual variations from firm standards.

3. How _active_ were you in practice development? What efforts did you make to bring in business for the firm? List speeches, articles, seminars, community, civic and charitable activities. How effective were they? What impact did they have?

4. Describe the <u>impact</u> of your efforts to build a ***team*** of professionals as opposed to practicing alone like a sole practitioner. Team activities would include bringing in other partners to meet your clients or provide services to them, bringing other firm members in to assist in managing client relationships, bringing other partners and/or staff to prospect meetings and networking activities and training others in areas of your expertise.

5. Summarize your performance in the following areas:

    a. The technical quality of your work

    b. Development of new markets, services, specialties

    c. Engagement management. Includes keeping your WIP to a minimum, maximizing realization, billing promptly, keeping your receivables to a reasonable level, etc.

    d. Retaining, developing, mentoring, nurturing and recruiting of staff. Explain the extent to which you feel you made a positive <u>impact</u> in these areas and what you did. List separately the names of staff and junior partners who have advanced and excelled in the firm under your tutelage.

    e. Living and breathing the firm's core values; promoting the firm's core values and leading people in these directions.

6. What have you done to ensure that your top five clients will remain with the firm if you should suddenly leave?

7. List the names of other firm members who have established meaningful relations ("touch points") with those top clients, thereby resulting in the client being a "firm" client rather than "your" client.

8. List any special accomplishments during the year that had a meaningful <u>impact</u> on the firm.

9. If your partners were asked to indicate areas of your performance this past year that needed improvement or were disappointing, what do you think they would say about you?

10. Performance of written goals. List your goals and indicate the extent to which the goals were accomplished. If the goals were not accomplished, indicate why and give a revised deadline. Use a separate page for this section.

11. Use this area to make any additional comments. Include comments necessary for your partners to get a good understanding of the kind of year you had.

10

Non-Binding Paper and Pencil Exercise Illustrated

Overview

The Paper and Pencil system is one method used by firms to allocate partner income. Each partner is given a sheet of paper (let's call it a ballot) that looks like this:

	Last Year	This Year
Partner A	320,000	
Partner B	410,000	
Partner C	280,000	
Partner D	250,000	
Partner E	350,000	
Partner F	320,000	
TOTAL	1,930,000	2,100,000

The left-hand column lists all the partners' names. The middle column shows the actual income allocation for the prior year. The right-hand column is blank except for the total amount of this year's partner income, which is the number each partner is asked to allocate, including to him/herself. This system essentially functions as a compensation committee consisting of all partners.

The critical importance of providing "voters" (the partners) with relevant data to review

The all-star team for major league baseball is determined by a vote of the fans. They simply fill out a ballot and submit it. Most voters spend just a few minutes on the ballot and do no research whatsoever on their choices.

This may be OK for the baseball all-star team, but it can be a disaster if the partners complete their ballots in 5 minutes based on their "gut feel." This is where a lot of firms make a mistake. Partners should only complete their ballot after reviewing the data, giving careful thought to their evaluations of each partner and then deciding the methodology they will use to allocate the income.

Attached to each ballot should be a comprehensive package of data that the partners should use to make their decisions. This package should be the same data that a compensation committee would review if one was in operation (see chapter 8).

Partners must allocate income based on objective information, not hearsay, reputations, past performance, friendships and jealousies.

Ground rules given to the partners

Firms have two choices:

1. No ground rules for the partners. They are free to allocate income using whatever system or methodology they choose. One partner could allocate income evenly, another could base it on their own "home-cooked" formula and still another could allocate income on ownership percentage. Free rein to the partners.

2. The firm gives the partners some ground rules. Examples could be:

- No one should allocate income on a pay-equal basis.
- For multi-office firms, allocate income based on the firm overall; don't try to link the income allocation to the profitability of each office.
- Don't use ownership percentage.

When the balloting is completed

When all partners have submitted their ballots, the numbers are averaged, and the resulting average for each partner is their allocated income number. Some firms eliminate the highest and lowest number for each partner before computing the average, for these reasons:

- The highest amount for a partner could be self-serving if it's the partners' own ballot.

- The lowest amount for a partner could result from one partner having a "vendetta" against another partner; there is no place in the system for this type of behavior.

- Even if the two above situations don't occur, eliminating the high and the low excludes extremes that could unfairly skew the results.

When the averages are computed, the firm can proceed in one of three directions:

1. The averages are final. No discussion. No appeal. That's it. Some refer to this sarcastically as the "chicken" method because the partners don't wish to engage in any group discussion regarding the fairness of the results. This avoids potentially unpleasant conversations.

2. The partner group discusses the results and the averages are modified if there is a consensus for doing so. Some refer to this as the "mature" method. The group has to decide what they will make available to each partner:

    a. All data showing how each partner voted, by partner. This obviously takes a lot of courage by the partner group. Some may feel that this defeats the purpose of the paper and pencil method because if partners know that their allocation for each partner will be seen by all other partners, they may not submit a ballot that is totally honest because they don't want to deal with the conflict that could result. I have observed this behavior at several firms.

    b. Just the final averages for each partner, with perhaps an indication of what the highest and lowest number was for each partner.

3. Similar to #2 above, the preliminary computation is sent to a compensation committee that may modify the numbers. Some firms require the committee to limit changes to a percentage of the tabulated average. Others give the committee free rein. Many compensation committees that use more collaborative methods to allocate income choose to have the partners complete the paper and pencil exercise but the results are totally non-binding to the committee.

Main justification for the paper and pencil method

If every partner completes a ballot in a fair, honest, forthright manner, what could be fairer than a system that determines each partner's income based on the collective wisdom of the each partner's value to the firm? It's hard to argue with this logic.

What number is actually allocated?

Two main options here:

1. Firms that have only one tier of income and partners receive a draw during the year. For these firms, the number to allocate would be total partner income excluding interest on capital.

2. For firms that have a base that is independent of the bonus, the exercise is done for both tiers. So, at the end of the year, the partners submit one ballot to allocate the bonus and another ballot to re-set the bases for the next year. Again, the numbers to allocate would exclude interest on capital.

What kinds of firm does the paper and pencil method appeal to?

1. Firms that don't like formulas.

2. The partners are comfortable with performance-based compensation, but aren't comfortable giving the responsibility for allocating income to a compensation committee or the managing partner.

3. Both of the above.

Pros and cons of the paper and pencil system

PROS

1. Potentially fewer arguments, especially if there are no discussions or appeals.

2. A good compromise for firms that want a performance-based system but aren't willing to trust a compensation committee or the managing partner.

CONS

1. As the partner group gets larger, it becomes very difficult for each partner to really know how <u>all</u> partners are performing. In a one office firm with 12 or fewer partners, most firms feel they are close enough to their partners to use this system. But once the partner count goes much beyond 12, usage of this system becomes more problematic.

2. It denies the firm's management, primarily the managing partner, from linking compensation with the performance of each partner as he/she observes it. The MP has no more say in compensation than any other partner. Knowing this, partners may not feel compelled to respond in an appropriate manner to the MP's attempts to hold them accountable for their performance.

3. This system tends to narrow the gap between highest and lowest paid partner, especially if highs and lows are eliminated before computing the average.

4. If there are "camps" or "cliques" of partners, this could skew the results.

5. Some partners, despite the requirement to study the data and observe the ground rules, complete their ballot using poor judgment.

Compiling the ballots

Several options for this:

1. Ballots are sent to the MP for tabulation.

2. Ballots sent to the COO/firm administrator for tabulation, who may provide the MP with overall averages or the details of each partner's ballot, depending on the methodology used.

3. Ballots sent to someone outside the firm such as a consultant or the firm's attorney.

As stated earlier, it's only natural for partners to submit their ballots differently depending on the extent that the details of their vote are seen by partners inside the firm such as the MP. Option #3 is the only way to ensure that partners cast they ballot with total openness and honesty.
Whoever reviews and tabulates the ballots should not limit their involvement to simply doing the math. They should also be doing certain things to help determine how *well* the system is working. When clients ask me to receive partner ballots and make the computation, I look for:

1. How often did a partner give him/herself the highest compensation? I always feel that if the system works well, relatively few partners give *themselves* the highest income.

2. How consistent are the votes? Specifically, how many partners out of the total submitted an income number that was within 10% of the average for each partner?

I feel that if the system works well, the votes should not have huge variations from high to low for each partner.

3. Did the partners follow the rules? Example: A few years ago, I worked with a seven partner firm that wanted to move from a modified pay-equal system to the paper and pencil system. When I reviewed the ballots, I saw that one partner allocated the income evenly to all seven partners. I called the partner and asked him why he did this. He apologized, said he made a mistake, and resubmitted his ballot. (To this day, I believe he lied to me and really wanted to allocate income evenly, but relented when I called him on it).

4. Did any partner's vote look strange? Example: One partner allocates an income number to a partner that is half of what she earned last year and half of what all the other partners voted. This partner needs to be asked why they did something so drastic to ensure that a mistake wasn't made.

Illustration

Assume that total partner income for the hypothetical firm illustrated below increased in 2014 to $1,010,000 from $925,000 in 2013.

UNADJUSTED (all numbers in thousands)

Assume that the partners' "votes" are as follows:

	2013	2014 Compensation Ballots						Pct.
		Mantle	Berra	Maris	Jeter	Ruth	Avg	Incr.
Mantle	225	250	235	240	220	290	247	9.8%
Berra	185	190	205	210	200	195	200	8.1%
Maris	200	205	215	225	220	215	216	8.0%
Jeter	175	205	205	190	205	190	199	13.7%
Ruth	140	160	150	145	165	120	148	5.7%
Total	925	1,010	1,010	1,010	1,010	1,010	1,010	9.2%

TAKE OUT THE HIGH AND LOW (all numbers in thousands)

If the high and low for each partner is eliminated before computing the average, here are the results:

		Mantle	Berra	Maris	Jeter	Ruth	Avg*	Incr
Mantle	225	250	235	240			241	7.2%
Berra	185		205		200	195	200	7.9%
Maris	200		215	225		215	218	9.0%
Jeter	175	205		190	205		200	14.1%
Ruth	140	160	150	145			151	8.2%
Total	925						1,010	9.2%

* Averages were ratcheted up to equal total income of $1,010,000.

11

Communication With The Partners

CPA firm partners, as all of us know, are very busy people. Communicating effectively with people, especially those within their own firm can be difficult simply because there never seems to be enough time to communicate properly with firm personnel.

This challenge is most certainly applicable to the compensation committee. The CC is composed of partners who lead very busy lives and have a full client load. As CC members, these partners take on an additional duty above and beyond their normal responsibilities. One can see how the time of the CC members would be stretched to the point where they don't have time to communicate their activities to the partners. If this is allowed to happen, it could spell the doom of the CC system.

Firms must understand that when the partners vote to use the CC system for allocating partner income, this is a huge leap of faith for them in terms of their comfort in trusting the CC to do its job fairly and objectively. They expect something in return. Partners want to know how the system works, how they will be evaluated and how the committee's judgment about their performance will lead directly to the income number they are allocated.

The two worst things a CC can do are:

1. Fail to make it clear to the partners how the system works.   As a result, the partners don't have a clue what they can do to earn more money.

2. Fail to spend time with the partners, both as a group and especially, one-on-one, to de-mystify the process of allocating income.

When CCs violate these taboos, this creates an image of a "smoke-filled back room" with power-hungry partners making critical decisions affecting partners' lives, feeling that they have no responsibility to explain their methods and decisions.

The operative word in this last sentence is "image." The CC members may in fact be neither "power-hungry" nor feel they are beyond culpability. But this is how the CC will be perceived by the partner group if they don't communicate effectively with the partners.

Three critical junctures in time that the CC must communicate to individual partners:

1. Just like in sports, principles of fairness state that the players must **understand the rules before the game begins**. This applies equally to partners in a firm using a CC to allocate income.

    At the beginning of the year, the CC should clearly communicate what will be expected of each partner by the end of the year and what criteria will be used to evaluate each partner's performance.

David Maister summed it up well: "Rules governing decisions must be consistent and well understood. Partners must understand which behaviors and what results translate the most to bigger rewards."

2. A fundamental tenet of goal setting is this: If one agrees on a set of goals on January 1 and **no one talks to the person about those goals until December 31**, it is unlikely that the goals will be accomplished.

   Throughout the year, the CC should monitor progress on each partner's goals. Ideally, this review should occur at least twice during the year.

3. **"Judgments that are explained and communicated are more readily accepted than those that are not."** (David Maister)

   After the year's end, the CC should communicate the final income numbers to each partner and explain how their number was determined: which aspects of their performance and behavior led to a higher allocation and what held their income back.

As stated in the beginning of this chapter, effective communication takes time. The CC members must understand that taking on the responsibility of serving on the CC will require a considerable time commitment. The CC members must be prepared for this.

12

Open vs. Closed Compensation Systems

In <u>open</u> compensation systems, all partners know what all other partners earn. In <u>closed</u> systems, only those involved in the allocation process know what all partners earn.

Theoretically, most of the seven major partner compensation systems can operate as closed systems, with a pay-equal system being the obvious exception. But for the most part, the concept of a closed compensation system is linked primarily with the compensation committee system, but also with the managing-partner-decides system.

80-90% of firms with fewer than 8 partners have open systems. But at firms with 13 or more partners, it's roughly 50-50.   80% or more of Top 100 firms' compensation systems are closed.

What explains this divergence?

It's an evolutionary phenomenon. Smaller firms hold dear their feelings of democracy. Partners in smaller firms have grown up with the firm and therefore, have always had access to all confidential data, including partner compensation details. Taking this "right" away initially seems incomprehensible. But as the firm grows larger and begins to be managed like a real business, it is neither feasible nor appropriate for partner compensation to be open.

Partners in smaller firms, at times, seem to compete with each other for their slice of the partner income pie. But as firms grow larger, partners come to understand that they should be compensated based on how they perform vs. *expectations*, not how they perform vs. *other partners*. A closed system gives the firm's management the freedom to link a partner's compensation to his/her performance without worrying about having to explain to Partner A why she was paid less than Partner B.

Reasons cited by partners for Open vs. Closed

Open	Closed
• Partners feel like "real" owners, privy to all confidential and sensitive data about the business they own.	• Let's get our partners to compete with *themselves*, not their partners.
• Avoids the image of a "smoke-filled room."	• The CC is less likely to be influenced by how they think partners will react to their income allocations.
• Access to fellow partners' paychecks allows us to see how we stack up.	• For a partner whose income isn't rising as fast as most of the others, it's depressing to see the new numbers every year. In a closed system, the lower income partners aren't as easily discouraged.
• Once a partner has had open access to other partners' comp, it's tough to take it away.	
• When a partner has access to all partners' comp, it enables him/her to judge the fairness and competence of the CC's decision making.	• A closed system makes it easier for the CC to recognize certain nuances that would be difficult to explain in an open environment. Example: a partner dealing with severe personal problems.

Think about it: Most corporations operate closed systems

A big part of the justification for adopting a closed compensation system is that this is the norm for the vast majority of corporations. With the minor exception of senior officers in publicly held businesses, whose compensation is required to be disclosed in statements to the SEC, compensation information about one's fellow officers is certainly not made accessible to all officers. Why should CPA firms be any different?

The experience of a new managing partner

Mitchell & Titus is a second generation firm, at or near the Top 100, based in New York, with offices in several major cities in the U.S. When MP Tony Kendall took office and became the firm's second ever CEO, he made some changes to the way the firm was managed. One of the changes had to do with partner compensation. Tony shared this at a conference:

"If you have an open compensation system, change it."

Tony shared this quote in the context of the firm fielding 34 years of complaints from partners on compensation issues.

Case study #1: Dealing with a cantankerous partner

I had helped this 10-partner firm change to a CC for the first time. I was asked to attend the CC's first meeting, as I frequently am, to guide the group through the process and keep it on track.

The firm had one long-time partner that had not only been under-performing for the past few years, but behaving in unacceptable ways such as refusing to talk with the MP, who admonished the mischievous partner for failing to collect his receivables.

When the two day CC meeting was nearing its end, the group did a very fine job of allocating income, which included a 2% increase for the problem partner's compensation while all others received increases that averaged 7%.

But after the initial allocations were agreed on, one member of the CC shouted out: "When we give Peter (name has been changed) his new compensation number and he sees that his increase was way smaller than all the other partners, he's going to go ballistic. Do we want to deal with this?"

The partners discussed it for an hour and decided that they did not wish to have a "war" on their hands. So, they gave Peter a slightly larger increase and slightly reduced the increases of certain other partners. If the firm had a closed system, the CC would have been less inclined to make this adjustment.

Case study #2: When partners elect a CC member who should not be on the committee

I was asked by an 11 partner firm to attend their CC meeting. A lot of time was spent discussing one partner in particular, who had severe performance issues. This partner not only had production-related deficiencies but interpersonal problems as well. This partner exhibited some strange behavior with several clients that led them to call the MP and lodge complaints. This partner was also abusive to staff on a few jobs. The discussion of this partner's evaluation was so serious that the CC debated whether or not to terminate the partner, deciding in the end to give the partner one more year to turn things around.

A month after this meeting, the firm held elections for the CC because one member was required to come off the committee due to a rule designed to give every partner a chance to serve on the CC. To the consternation of the CC, the partner group, seven of whom were blissfully unaware of this partner's serious shortcomings, elected the problem partner to the committee!

I advised the MP that he must find a way to prevent this problem partner from serving on the CC because it violates a fundamental principle of operating an effective CC: All partners must be credible in the eyes of the partner group.

The MP convened a meeting of the previous CC to get their support for overruling the election results, which he was able to do. Next, he met with a few other influential partners and obtained their support as well. Armed with the support of a strong majority of his partners, the MP never made public the fact that (1) this problem partner was elected to the CC and that (2) he overruled the election of the problem partner. The partner who garnered the next highest amount of votes became a member of the new CC.

The lessons to be learned from this:

1. Don't prevent effective CC members from serving continuous terms.   If the person is doing a good job, and the partners wish to re-elect him/her, the firm shouldn't have any problems with this. By adopting a rule that every partner should get a turn on the CC, a firm risks that that eventually, a partner will get elected to the CC who is not credible in the eyes of the other partners.

2. As much as partners love the concept of democracy, they should consider practices to ensure that the CC is always comprised of highly credible partners, even at the risk of slightly reducing the element of democracy to the process. Two such practices are:

    a. Have heavy overlap between the executive and compensation committee. Don't allow your zeal for democratic elections to prevent EC members from serving on the CC.

    b. If the partners feel strongly that there should at least be one member of the CC that is not an EC member, let the MP appoint the extra person rather than do this by election.

    c. If the partners are not comfortable with letting the MP appoint the extra CC member, restrict the election to one member of the CC.

13

Timetable for the Compensation Committee

Here is an example for the timetable for a calendar year-end firm:

Action Item	General Timeline	Actual Dates
1. Election of compensation committee (CC) members. The earlier, the better.	Feb. 15 – Oct. 1	
2. Decide what 12-month period will be evaluated: Calendar? 11/1 to 10/31? Etc.	Feb. 15 – Oct. 1	
3. Decide if the system will be open or closed.	Feb. 15 – Oct. 1	
4. Create/update the firm's strategic plan and vision. The firm needs to decide where it wants to go so the partners know what is needed from them, and therefore, what should be rewarded.	Any time in advance of goal setting process	
5. Partners draft their goals for next year.	Nov. 1	
6. Self-evaluation forms distributed to the partners.	Dec. 1	
7. Partners complete their self-evaluations, which include a written summary of their progress toward annual goals.	Dec. 10	

Action Item	General Timeline	Actual Dates
8. CC meets with each partner to finalize the goals for the *coming year* and to ensure that partner goals are aligned with the firm's strategic plan and vision.	Dec. 10-Jan. 10	
9. Communicate clearly to each partner what his/her role is in the firm going forward and what is expected of him/her in the coming year.	Dec. 10–Jan. 10	
10. The CC, MP or others meet individually with each partner to review their performance for the year just ended.	Dec. 10–Jan. 10	
11. If the base and bonus are independent of each other, decide what the size of the base and bonus pools will be for the coming year, as a percent of total income.	Dec. 10-Jan. 10	
12. Key members of the firm's management, such as PICs and department heads who are not members of the CC, should communicate their feedback on the partners to the CC.	Jan. 1–Jan. 15	
13. Information to be collected and reviewed by the CC (list not all-inclusive): production statistics, achievement of written goals, performance evaluations (self-evaluations, upward, peer evaluations by other partners), MP and PIC opinions.	Jan. 15	

Action Item	General Timeline	Actual Dates
14. Optional: Conduct a non-binding paper and pencil exercise. Be sure to distribute relevant documentation to the partners along with the ballots.	Send out Jan. 15 Back by Jan. 20	
15. CC decides the size of the base and bonus tiers for next year.	Jan. 22- Feb. 10	
16. CC meets to finalize evaluations and make the income allocations. If the base and bonus are independent, the CC needs to finalize bonus for the year just concluded, and to set next year's base. If the base is really an advance on a final number that the bonus adjusts, finalize this year's total income numbers and set next year's partner draws. You may need two separate meetings; one for completing overall evaluations and one for allocating the income.	Jan. 22- Feb. 10	
17. Communication of the income allocation results to the partners. This will either be for the base *and* bonus or just the bonus.	Feb. 10-20	
18. Communicate to the partners what criteria will be used by the CC in making its allocation decisions for the year ahead. What performance and behavior will have a higher impact and what will have a lower impact?	Feb. 10-20	
19. During the year, each partner's goals should be monitored and reviewed.	During the year	

14

Best Practices for Compensation Committees

1. The partners must understand the heart and soul of the Compensation Committee (CC) approach: The system can only work if the people being judged are willing to <u>trust the judges</u>. Period. If the partners aren't comfortable with this, then they should not use the CC.

2. CC = Executive Committee (EC).

3. <u>Make-up</u> of the committee:
    *   Should be small; for one-office firms, no more than 3-5 people is sufficient.
    *   MP is a permanent member.
    *   If a CC is separate from the EC, CC members *other than* the MP should be <u>appointed</u> if there are partners with significant management duties such as PICs of large offices and department heads that truly manage other partners. Otherwise, elections should be held.
    *   <u>Every</u> member of the CC must be credible in the eyes of the other partners.
    *   No mandatory rotation.
    *   Minimal limits on CC members serving multiple terms.
    *   Stagger the terms of CC members so that there is continuity from year to year.

4. It should be clear to each partner what his/her <u>role in the firm is and what is expected</u> of him/her. Each partner should have a set of formal, written goals.

5. The CC has <u>full reign</u> in deciding the methods and techniques used to allocate income. Their mandate is to achieve a <u>balance between production and intangibles.</u>

6. The partner compensation system should be <u>closed</u> instead of open. Partners should be given general information on where they stand vs. other partners, but no specifics on what individual partners earn.

7. <u>Link of compensation with the firm's strategic plan and vision</u>. Partners do what the firm *needs* them to do.

8. <u>Performance criteria</u> (no significance to this order):
    *   Each partner has formal, written, SMART goals.
    *   Major performance attributes identified; not the same for each partner. These attributes should include many of the following:
        i.   Leadership.
        ii. People skills including effective staff mentoring.
        iii. Practice development.
        iv. Building strong teams beneath you.
        v.   Traditional production (client base, billable hours, realization, etc.)
        vi. Great client service.
        vii. Good citizenship (adhering to the firm's policies, procedures and practices; living and breathing the firm's core values).

9. Partner compensation should consist of <u>three tiers</u>: Interest on accrual basis capital, base salary and incentive bonus.

10. The <u>base and bonus should be mutually exclusive</u>.

- The base should represent the "street value" of each partner and their worth to the firm, influenced by the cumulative size of production metrics such as business originated and size of client base managed.
- The bonus should focus on the <u>current year</u>, based on achievement of goals, intangibles, and in general, what each partner did to cause the firm to have a good year or a bad year (what have you done for us lately?).

If the firm does not have clear, written goals and expectations for the performance of each partner, then the base should be a draw on a final income number and the bonus should be a final distribution that adjusts the draw to that final number.

11. The CC should make a sincere effort to carefully <u>review all pertinent information</u> necessary to assess each partner's performance. Feedback from management personnel that are <u>not</u> CC members should be obtained. This group includes office PICs, department heads, and high level internal personnel such as the COO, marketing director and HR director.

12. If a firm has one office with 10 or fewer partners, the CC should conduct a <u>Paper and Pencil exercise</u>. The results are <u>non-binding</u> to the CC and should only be done if the CC feels this exercise will be useful to them. Results should not be revealed in any way to the partners.

13. <u>Calendar year firms</u> must decide the 12 month period of time that will be used to collect data. Typically, CC members are heavily immersed in the tax season during the crucial period of time that performance data must be reviewed, deliberations take place and communications with each partner completed. To avoid this conflict, the data should be <u>collected on a twelve months ended</u>

<u>September 30 basis</u> with all of the CC's work completed by December 31.

14. Income numbers for each partner should be finalized by the CC. This should be done in a way that resists the temptation to reduce everything to a formula. Instead, a process of discussion should be used to finalize the income allocations.

    CC must make <u>two decisions</u>:
    - Finalize bonus/year-end distribution for the year just ended.
    - Set bases/draws for next year.

15. <u>Communication</u> at 3 critical points in the year:

    - At the <u>beginning of the year</u>, the CC should clearly communicate what will be expected of each partner by the end of the year and how their performance will be evaluated by the CC. Being clear on the "rules" <u>before</u> the game begins.
    - <u>Throughout the year,</u> the CC should monitor progress. Unless there is communication between the CC and the partners during the year, it's unlikely that the partners' goals will be achieved.
    - <u>After the year's end,</u> the CC should communicate the final income numbers to each partner and explain how their number was determined. Judgments explained are more readily accepted than those that are not.

16. <u>Decisions</u> of the CC should be <u>final</u>. No appeals. No approval by the full partner group.

15

Challenges for the Compensation Committee

How many management practices in <u>any</u> line of business or organization are perfect? Very few and probably none. Running a compensation committee is not a perfect solution to allocating partner income by any stretch. But it's the best we have.

Here are six challenges for compensation committees:

1. How do the CC members set their own compensation?

There are two alternatives and I've seen both used with regularity: At some firms, when it comes time for the committee to discuss a CC member, the group asks the individual to step outside of the room. Other committees have no problem discussing the performance and income allocation for each partner in front of each other.

This is something that cannot be dictated or mandated. It's really up to the CC members themselves and their comfort level with the two options.

2. **How do CC members handle the situation in which they end up being the highest paid partners?**

This is <u>extremely</u> common because the highest performers are very often the most credible partners in the firm and partners feel very comfortable putting compensation decisions in their hands.

Nonetheless, things can get awkward for the CC members. They worry that making themselves the highest paid partners or awarding themselves the highest bonuses will be seen as self-serving and will send the wrong message to the partners.

It's testimony to the legendary integrity and humility of CPA firm partners that the main way CC members deal with this issue is to err on the side of giving themselves slightly less money than they deserve. I have seen this repeatedly throughout my consulting career.

In my experience, the other partners understand that the CC members are often the firm's top performers, and they expect them to be the highest paid. The evidence of their excellence is clear to everyone.

3. **Don't CCs eventually have to use *some sort* of formula to allocate the income?**

No, no and no, in that order!

The beauty of the compensation committee system is that CC members are not shackled to any mechanical, robot-like methodology. They are free to search their hearts and their minds to use their good judgment, formed after careful, time-consuming analysis, to allocate income.

New CCs, especially those coming off a formula system, have a tough time with this challenge to avoid the use of formulas. **Also, their education and experience as accountants makes them** comfortable with formulas, despite their decision to abandon them!

4. **Avoiding the image of the "smoke-filled" room.**

We have addressed this throughout this monograph, but it bears repeating. It is undoubtedly one of the biggest challenges for CCs. The committee members must commit the time necessary to do the job "right." And doing the job "right" means spending lots of time communicating with the partners (a) at the *beginning* of the year to establish the "rules of the game," (b) *during* the year to convey the message that they are "watching" what the partners are doing and (c) at the *end* of the year to make it crystal clear how each partner's pay was determined.

5. **Dealing with "problem partners."**

What are "problem partners?" We all know them. Here are two examples:

- A problem partner could be a rainmaker and/or have one of the biggest client bases. This makes them feel they are entitled to commit every transgression in the book, especially being curt and nasty to partners and staff alike, without fear of discipline.
- The partners are reluctant to address these shortcomings for fear that it may drive the partner out of the firm, which if this happens, could have a significant impact on their future income.

- A problem partner never can keep his/her head above water. Billing and collections always late. Arriving late to partner meetings and leaving early. Timesheets late. Major client projects planned at the last minute, causing staff to be pulled off jobs that *were* planned in advance. Their office is a disaster area. They seem to be in a rut that they can't get out of.

Most firms have problem partners. How should the CC deal with these people? In the case of ferocious rainmakers, it takes a lot of courage by the CC to impact the pay of these partners and risk a war that could result in their departure from the firm.   In the other cases, the CC has to be willing to send a clear message that the status quo is not acceptable. In short, it requires "tough love." It's never easy and will always challenge the CC. But it has to be done for the good of the firm.

6.   Should the Executive Committee be the same as the Compensation Committee?

Yes, absolutely, as we explained in Chapter 5.

Firms need to fight the urge to allow democracy to pervade every aspect of the firm's governance. If the partners expect the firm to be well managed, then there needs to be partner accountability. Professional service firms like CPA and law firms are notorious for resembling the herding of cats. Richard Ungaretti, founder of a prestigious law firm in Chicago, is famous for this analogy:

"When a corporation says move left, everybody takes a step left. In a partnership, when you say move left, three people go to the bathroom, four people move right and five people leave the firm."

If the firm's management, which includes the executive committee, is expect to hold partners accountable for their performance and behavior, then it needs to link performance with compensation. Denying the firm's management the authority to make this linkage makes it almost impossible to achieve partner accountability.

Firms need to get away from any image in their minds that a CC is a short-term activity than happens once a year for a few days. CCs should not be empaneled like juries; <u>effective</u> CCs function as permanent, year-round bodies that take their role in the firm's management very seriously.

20733867R00068

Made in the USA
Middletown, DE
06 June 2015